EXTREME SPORTS
An Imagination Library Series

D0689994

SKYDIVING

by John E. Schindler

GARETH**STEVENS**
PUBLISHING
A WRC Media Company

Please visit our web site at: www.garethstevens.com
For a free color catalog describing Gareth Stevens Publishing's
list of high-quality books and multimedia programs,
call 1-800-542-2595 (USA) or 1-800-387-3178 (Canada).
Gareth Stevens Publishing's fax: (414) 332-3567.

Library of Congress Cataloging-in-Publication Data available upon request from publisher.
Fax (414) 336-0157 for the attention of the Publishing Records Department.

ISBN 0-8368-4543-9 (lib. bdg.)
ISBN 0-8368-4550-1 (softcover)

First published in 2005 by
Gareth Stevens Publishing
A WRC Media Company
330 West Olive Street, Suite 100
Milwaukee, WI 53212 USA

Text: John E. Schindler
Cover design and page layout: Tammy West
Series editor: Carol Ryback
Photo research: Diane Laska-Swanke

Photo credits: Cover, pp. 5, 7, 9, 11, 13, 15, 17, 19, 21 © Tony Hathaway

Printed in the United States of America

1 2 3 4 5 6 7 8 9 09 08 07 06 05

Cover: A student skydiver (center) takes
her first accelerated free fall with the help
of two instructors.

TABLE OF CONTENTS

Words that appear in the glossary are printed in **boldface**
type the first time they occur in the text.

DIVING INTO THE SKY

Have you ever thought about floating in the air? Skydivers do it every day. They jump from an airplane, open up their **parachutes**, and float to the ground.

All skydivers travel one way — down! But there is more than one way to skydive. Some skydivers open their parachutes as they leave the airplane. Other skydivers **free-fall** hundreds of feet before opening their parachutes.

Groups of skydivers might do tricks as they free-fall. They sometimes hook together in the sky. When they hook up while falling, it is called a **free-fall formation**. The biggest free-fall formation ever included 357 skydivers hooked together!

A skydiver waves at the camera after jumping from an airplane. He will fall through the air for a few more seconds before opening his parachute.

A DOG TAKES THE LEAD

The first living thing to parachute was not a person. In 1785, someone dropped a dog from a hot-air balloon. The dog sat in a basket that hung from a parachute. He landed safely.

People parachuted from hot-air balloons before airplanes were invented. Parachuting from airplanes became very important during **World War II**. Special soldiers called **paratroopers** used parachutes to reach battles.

Skydiving became a sport in the 1950s. Schools and clubs for skydiving started up near airports around the world. Now people can learn to skydive no matter where they live. They must be at least sixteen years old.

Soldier skydivers, called paratroopers, used round parachutes during World War II.

SCHOOL GROUNDS

You have probably fallen down sometime. It just happens. You do not think about it. All of a sudden, you land on the ground.

Falling and landing with a parachute is different. A skydiving instructor shows students how to fall from an airplane. She also teaches them the safe way to land on the ground.

Do these lessons happen high in the clouds? No! Beginning skydivers take most of their classes on solid ground.

Some skydiving schools have a low **jump tower** for practicing jumping and landing. Skydivers learn how to land a parachute in a practice field.

Soon they go up, up, and away!

A skydiving student practices how to land and fall to the ground without getting hurt.

DROP BY SOMETIME

Ready for your first skydiving jump? Put on your **jumpsuit** and get into the airplane. The instructor in charge of the jump is called the jumpmaster. He reviews the safety rules for skydiving. Listen up!

Soon the airplane flies over the landing zone. The jump door opens. It becomes very loud on the plane.

Your jumpmaster uses a hand signal to tell you when to jump. You must move near the open door and wait your turn. Will you be first or last?

Wait for the signal — then jump! Everything becomes very peaceful after your parachute opens. You float down to Earth quietly.

A skydiver gets ready to jump from an airplane. He carries his parachute in the backpack.

JUMP STARTS

Some instructors let you choose how to do your first jump. You might choose a **static line** jump. A static line is a metal rope, or cable, that is hooked to the airplane. It opens the parachute as you jump.

A **tandem** jump is another popular jump for beginners. Tandem means two at once. You and your instructor are tied together. You float down together using one parachute.

If you dare, you might choose an **accelerated free fall** for your first jump. This means that two instructors jump out of the airplane with you. They stay near you until you pull your **ripcord**. The ripcord is a cord you pull to open your parachute.

Awesome!

Some people take a tandem skydive to see what skydiving is all about before they sign up for lessons.

GEAR UP TO FALL

Skydiving gear includes a main parachute and a secondary, or reserve, parachute. The main chute is the parachute that normally opens in a dive. You must use the reserve chute if the main chute does not work right.

A **harness** attaches the parachute to your body. An **altimeter** attaches to your harness or to your wrist. The altimeter measures how high you are above the ground.

Your jumpsuit covers all your clothes. Cloth "wings" on the jumpsuit may help you steer during free fall. A jumpsuit also helps block the wind and keeps you warm. Your helmet and goggles protect your head and eyes.

These skydivers are almost set to jump! Each wears a parachute harness, jumpsuit, and helmet. They will all need to wear goggles for the jump.

KIND OF A DRAG

The colorful cloth part of a parachute is called the **canopy**. It opens up to catch air. The open canopy slows the person's fall. The slowing down caused by the canopy is called **drag**.

You steer a parachute by pulling on control lines. You pull on the right control line to go right. A pull on the left control line makes you go left.

You can steer more toward one direction to take a better look at something. Steering the parachute is easier when you are higher. You must steer more carefully as you get closer to the ground.

A paratrooper pulls on his parachute lines as he drops down for a soft landing.

TARGET PRACTICE

Many skydivers like to enter contests. One of their favorite contests is to steer toward a small target on the ground. The skydiver who lands exactly on the target wins.

Some skydivers also like an exciting new sport. They "sky surf" with a **sky board**. A sky board looks like a snowboard. A sky surfer jumps out of an airplane with the sky board attached to his feet. He uses the sky board to help him do tricks such as somersaults and upside-down spins.

Sky surfers are judged on their style and form. A sky surfer drops his sky board before he lands. It might get in his way!

A skydiver lands almost on his target.

THE FUTURE OF SKYDIVING

You can take skydiving lessons when you get older. Every skydiving school has an age rule. Check with your local skydiving training center to learn its rules for beginners.

Skydivers enjoy the feeling of falling through the air and making formations. They can sky surf. They can land on tiny targets.

Skydivers like to find new things to do as they drop through the air. Most of the extreme ways to skydive started in the last few years.

What will skydivers do next? You might be the person to invent a new way to dive the skies!

Skydivers sometimes like to link up in a colorful formation in the air before opening their parachutes.

MORE TO READ AND VIEW

Books (Nonfiction) The *Golden Knights: The U.S. Army Parachute Team. Serving Your Country* (series). Ellen H. Hopkins. (Capstone)

Sky Surfing. Extreme Sports (series). Patrick Ryan. (Capstone)

Skydiving! Take the Leap. The Extreme Sports Collection (series). Jeremy Roberts. (Rosen)

Skysurfing. High Interest Book: X-Treme Outdoors (series). Holly Cefrey. (Children's Press)

Team Skydiving. Charles and Linda George. (Capstone)

Books (Fiction) *My Life as a Screaming Skydiver. The Incredible Worlds of Wally McDoogle: #14.* Bill Myers. (Thomas Nelson, Inc.)

DVDs and Videos *Ripcord: A Wild and Exhilarating Ride!* (2000). (Goldhil Home Media)

Skydiving: Ultimate Thrill. (Simitar Entertainment)

WEB SITES

Web sites change frequently, but the following web sites should last awhile. You can also search Google (*www.google.com*) or Yahooligans! (*www.yahooligans.com*) for more information about skydiving. Some keywords to help your search include: *free fall, Golden Knights, hot-air balloons, parachutes, paratroopers, ripcord, sky surfing, skydiving, static line jumping, tandem skydiving.*

www.airspeed.org/main_index.htm
Visit the Arizona Airspeed skydiving team's web site and see how they do in global competitions.

www.enclave.com/cgilocal/if/ imagefolio.cgi?direct=World_Free fall_convention
View images of skydivers from around the world. Includes links to other skydiving categories such as tandem and freestyle.

www.skydiveworld.com/english/ games.htm
Play all the fun online skydiving games! Requires Shockwave.

www.uspa.org/
Official site of the United States Parachuting Association, featuring information for both beginning and advanced skydivers. Explore the list of official skydiving records, parachuting competitions, and skydiving clubs.

GLOSSARY

You can find these words on the pages listed. Reading a word in a sentence helps you understand it even better.

accelerated free fall — a fall through the air with two instructors before opening your parachute. Beginners might do this. 12

altimeter (awl-TIM-it-er) — an instrument that measures how high an object is. 14

canopy — the part of the parachute that fills with air. 16

free fall — falling several minutes before your parachute opens. 4, 12, 16,

free-fall formation — skydivers hooking up to form a shape as they fall. 4, 20

harness — straps that attach an object to another object. 14

jump tower — a low tower used for teaching skydivers how to land. 8

jumpsuit — a one-piece suit worn over clothing, usually for protection. 10, 14

parachutes — umbrella-shaped devices that open up to catch air and slow down a fall. 4, 6, 8, 10, 12, 14, 16

paratroopers — soldiers trained to parachute into battle. 6

ripcord — a cord that opens a parachute. 12

sky board — a short board for doing air tricks. 18

static line — a cable hooked to the airplane that opens your parachute as you jump into the air. 12

tandem — built for two. 12

World War II — the largest war in history, fought between 1939 and 1945. 6

INDEX